Fact Finders™

The American Colonies

The Connecticut Colony

by Muriel L. Dubois

Consultant:
Jon Emmett Purmont
Professor, Department of History
Southern Connecticut State University
New Haven, Connecticut

Capstone
press

Mankato, Minnesota

Fact Finders is published by Capstone Press,
151 Good Counsel Drive, P.O. Box 669, Mankato, Minnesota 56002.
www.capstonepress.com

Library of Congress Cataloging-in-Publication Data
Dubois, Muriel L.
　　The Connecticut colony / by Muriel L. Dubois.
　　p. cm. — (Fact Finders. American colonies)
　　Includes index.
　　ISBN 0–7368–2672–6 (hardcover)
　　1. Connecticut—History—Colonial period, ca. 1600–1775—Juvenile literature.　I. Title.
II. Series: American colonies (Capstone Press)
F97.D83 2006
974.6'02—dc22　　　　　　　　　　　　　　　　　　　　　　　2004029361

Summary: An introduction to the history, government, economy, resources, and people of
　　the Connecticut Colony.　Includes maps and charts.

Editorial Credits
Mandy Marx, editor; Jennifer Bergstrom, set designer, illustrator, and book designer;
　　Bobbi J. Dey, book designer; Jo Miller, photo researcher/photo editor

Photo Credits
Cover image: Thomas Hooker and Congregation offering thanks on their arrival in
　　Connecticut in 1636. The Granger Collection, New York.

Corbis/Bettmann, 18
The Granger Collection, New York, 10, 12–13, 16–17, 20–21
Marilyn "Angel" Wynn, 4–5
Mary Evans Picture Library, 7
North Wind Picture Archives, 6, 11, 14, 22, 23, 26, 27, 29 (both)

1 2 3 4 5 6 10 09 08 07 06 05

Table of Contents

Chapter 1

Connecticut's First People

The Connecticut River Valley was once home to many American Indians. Several Algonquian tribes lived there. They included the Pequot, Podunk, and Mohegan people.

Algonquian Daily Life

Connecticut's Algonquian tribes lived off the land around them. Their homes were called wetus or wigwams. To make a home, men stood tree saplings in a circle. They bent the tops toward the center and tied them. Women made mats of bark or plants to cover the tops. The Algonquian also made tools from things they found in nature.

The Algonquian used spears made of wood, rock, and bone to hunt animals.

For food, the Algonquian hunted, fished, and farmed. Men hunted deer, moose, turkeys, and other local animals. In summer, they fished in the ocean or in Connecticut's rivers. Everyone helped plant corn, beans, and squash. Women picked the crops when they were ready. They also gathered nuts and berries in the forests.

Picking corn was a big job. Many people pitched in to make the work easier. ▼

At first, each town ruled itself. In 1638, they formed a central government. Under Hooker's leadership, the Connecticut colonists wrote the Fundamental Orders. This **constitution** set up the government of Connecticut. It let people in each town vote for **representatives** to make laws. The colony as a whole elected a governor.

In 1638, another group from Massachusetts began the New Haven Colony. This colony was located on what is now Connecticut's southern coast. In 1664, New Haven joined the Connecticut Colony.

F A C T !

Connecticut is called "The Constitution State." The Fundamental Orders was the first constitution written in North America.

Connecticut colonists were proud to take part in their government. ▼

~ Chapter 3 ~
Colonial Life

The first Connecticut colonists faced many difficulties. Settlers had to clear land to build homes and farms. Their first shelters were made of sticks and mud. Later, they built small wooden houses.

For most families, life centered around the farm. Connecticut settlers planted corn, pumpkins, and beans. They also picked wild blueberries, strawberries, and nuts.

Everyone had their own job to do. Men took care of the farm. Women took care of the home. Children helped their parents with daily chores.

Most Connecticut colonists lived and worked on farms.

Fighting for Land

At first, the colonists got along well with most of Connecticut's Indians. In 1637, they helped several tribes fight the Pequot War (1636–1637). Together, they defeated the Pequots.

But as more settlers came, they stole Indian land. This angered the Indians, so they attacked the colonists. Soon, fights between settlers and Indians were common.

Connecticut colonists also fought the French. France had colonies to the north and west of the British colonies in North America.

◄ During the Pequot War, English settlers destroyed entire Pequot villages.

From 1689 to 1763, the British fought the French for their land in North America. Many American Indians sided with the French. These battles are now called the French and Indian wars.

In 1763, the colonists helped the British defeat the French and the Indians. By winning, Britain controlled all of the land east of the Mississippi River.

Population Growth of the Connecticut Colony

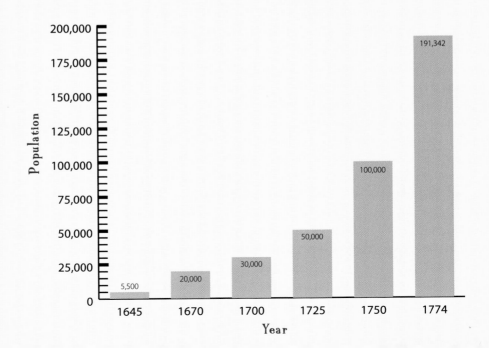

Chapter 4

Work and Trade

As Connecticut settlements grew into towns and cities, people's lives changed. Colonists didn't have to farm to survive. Merchants built stores. Wagon makers, blacksmiths, and shoemakers opened shops. Shipbuilders made ships for ocean or river travel.

Connecticut was famous for manufacturing. Gristmills ground grain into flour. Sawmills cut logs into lumber. Foundries melted and molded raw metal into useful hardware. Craftsmen made iron, brass, and tin into shoe buckles, candlestick holders, and tools. Workers in Connecticut also made the first brass buttons in the American colonies.

Tinsmiths pounded and shaped tin into many useful items.

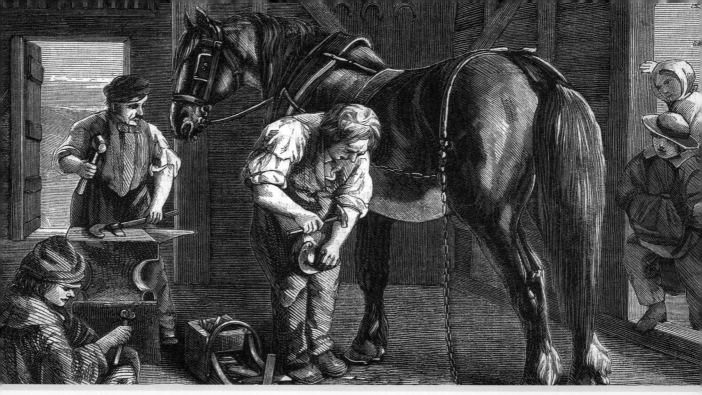

Unpaid Labor

Many workers in Connecticut did not earn money. Some people worked to learn a skill. Others did it as a way to get to America. Some simply had no choice.

Apprentices worked with craftsmen to learn a trade or skill. The usual length of service was seven years. Then the craftsman gave the apprentice clothes, tools, or money to start a business.

▲ Blacksmiths learned their skills as apprentices.

Poor people came to America as **indentured servants**. Local settlers paid for their passage. The settler owned the servant until he or she worked off the debt.

Some Connecticut colonists kept slaves. Most slaves were from Africa, but some were American Indians. Slaves could never leave their owners. They were arrested and punished if they ran away.

In 1784, Connecticut passed laws to free the children of slaves. In 1848, Connecticut's government finally made slavery against the law.

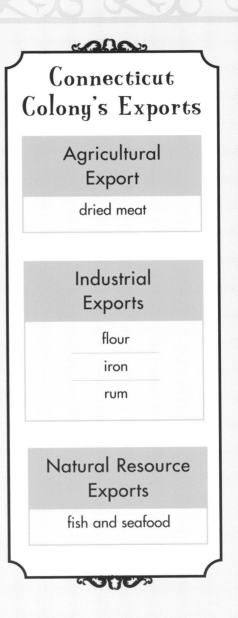

Connecticut Colony's Exports

Agricultural Export

dried meat

Industrial Exports

flour

iron

rum

Natural Resource Exports

fish and seafood

Chapter 5

Community and Faith

Most of the people in Connecticut were Puritans. Their faith centered around reading the Bible. For this reason, learning to read was important in Connecticut. In 1650, Connecticut passed a law about education. It said towns with 50 families or more must have schools.

Connecticut towns were built around the meetinghouse. On Sundays, church services were held in this building. The meetinghouse also served as a town hall for meetings and elections.

Connecticut colonists valued higher education. Yale University was founded in Connecticut in 1701.

Ruling Themselves

Many Connecticut colonists had come from Massachusetts. There, church leaders ran the government. Connecticut colonists wanted a different government. They set up a government led by the people. In 1662, King Charles II granted the colony its **charter**. It allowed the Connecticut colonists to rule themselves.

Connecticut colonists had town meetings to make laws in a fair way. ▼

The Charter Oak

In 1682, England's King James II wanted all of New England to be one colony. He sent Sir Edmund Andros to govern New England. Andros reached Connecticut on October 31, 1687. He had come to get the charter.

A group of Connecticut colonists met with Andros. During the meeting, the candles in the room went out. In the dark, a colonist named Joseph Wadsworth snuck out with the charter. He hid it in a hollow oak tree. Without the charter, Andros did not have the power to rule Connecticut.

▲ The story of the Charter Oak is part of Connecticut's proud history.

FACT!

Sir Andros ruled New England from 1686 to 1689. Connecticut was the only New England colony to keep self-rule.

Chapter 6

Becoming a State

By 1763, the American colonies had busy cities and large farms. Connecticut also had many factories. Some people thought the colonies were outgrowing Britain's rule.

At this time, Britain put **taxes** on paper, sugar, and tea. Connecticut colonists were used to having a voice in their government. They didn't think Britain should tax them, since they had no say in British government.

In September 1774, the colonies sent representatives to the Continental Congress. These men tried to come to an agreement with Great Britain. But their efforts at peace failed.

Connecticut was a New England Colony. It was one of the first colonies to demand independence. ➡

The Thirteen Colonies, 1763

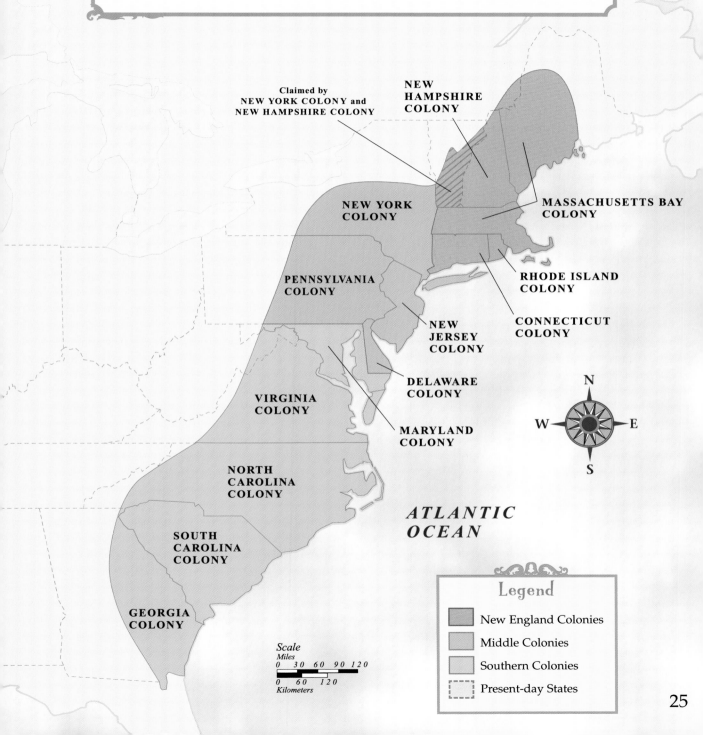

Claimed by
NEW YORK COLONY and
NEW HAMPSHIRE COLONY

NEW HAMPSHIRE COLONY

NEW YORK COLONY

MASSACHUSETTS BAY COLONY

PENNSYLVANIA COLONY

RHODE ISLAND COLONY

NEW JERSEY COLONY

CONNECTICUT COLONY

DELAWARE COLONY

VIRGINIA COLONY

MARYLAND COLONY

NORTH CAROLINA COLONY

SOUTH CAROLINA COLONY

GEORGIA COLONY

ATLANTIC OCEAN

N
W   E
S

Scale
Miles
0   30   60   90   120

0   60   120
Kilometers

Legend
New England Colonies
Middle Colonies
Southern Colonies
Present-day States

25

▲ Connecticut men were eager to volunteer as soldiers in the Revolutionary War.

FACT!

The Battle at Groton-New London was the only major Revolutionary War battle in Connecticut. The British won.

The Road to Freedom

In 1775, the Revolutionary War broke out. Congress approved the Declaration of **Independence** in July 1776. It said the American colonies were states, free of British rule.

Connecticut colonists played an important role in the war. They served as soldiers. They also gave the army food and supplies. In 1783, America won the war.

Forming a Nation

In 1787, American leaders wrote the United States Constitution. It created the U.S. government. Each state elected representatives who could vote on laws.

State leaders argued over how many representatives to have. Small states wanted an equal number. Large states wanted more. Connecticut's leaders had the solution.

The Connecticut Compromise made laws pass through two houses. All states had two representatives in the Senate. Large states had more in the House of Representatives. On January 9, 1788, Connecticut became the fifth state to approve the U.S. Constitution.

Connecticut's leaders helped set up the U.S. government. ▼

Fast Facts

Name

The Connecticut Colony (named after Mohegan word meaning "Beside the long tidal river")

Location

New England

Dates of Founding

1633–1636

First Settlements

Windsor, Wethersfield, Hartford

Colony's Founder

Thomas Hooker

Religious Faith

Puritan

Agricultural Product

Dried meat

Major Industry

Manufacturing

Population in 1774

191,342 people

Statehood

January 9, 1788 (5th state)

Time Line

1664
New Haven
Colony joins the
Connecticut Colony.

1662
King Charles II of England
grants the Connecticut
Colony its charter.

1638
Connecticut adopts the
Fundamental Orders.

1633-1636
Colonists from Massachusetts start
the towns of Windsor, Wethersfield,
and Hartford; they join and form
the Connecticut Colony.

1689-1763
Great Britain and
France fight over
land in North
America; these
wars are called
the French and
Indian wars.

1707
An Act of Union
unites England,
Wales, and
Scotland; they
become the
Kingdom of
Great Britain.

1763
Proclamation of
1763 sets colonial
borders and
provides land for
American Indians.

1776
Declaration of
Independence is
approved in July.

1783
America wins
Revolutionary War.

1775
American colonies begin
fight for independence
from Great Britain in the
Revolutionary War.

1788
On January 9th,
Connecticut is the fifth
state to join the
United States.

29

Glossary

charter (CHAR-tur)—an official document that grants permission to create a colony and provides for a government

constitution (kon-stuh-TOO-shuhn)—the written system of laws in a state or country that state the rights of the people and the powers of the government

democratic (dem-uh-KRAT-ik)—a type of government where people vote for their leaders

indentured servant (in-DEN-churd SUR-vuhnt)—someone who agrees to work for another person for a certain length of time in exchange for travel expenses, food and housing

independence (in-di-PEN-duhnss)—the condition of being free from the control of other people

Puritan (PYOOR-uh-tuhn)—one of a group of Protestants who sought simple church services and a strict moral code

representative (rep-ri-ZEN-tuh-tiv)—someone who is chosen to speak or act for others

taxes (TAKS-uhs)—money that people and businesses must pay to support a government

Internet Sites

FactHound offers a safe, fun way to find Internet sites related to this book. All of the sites on FactHound have been researched by our staff.

Here's how:

1. Visit *www.facthound.com*
2. Type in this special code **0736826726** for age-appropriate sites. Or enter a search word related to this book for a more general search.
3. Click on the **Fetch It** button.

FactHound will fetch the best sites for you!

Read More

Burgan, Michael. *The Connecticut Colony.* Our Thirteen Colonies. Chanhassen, Minn.: Child's World, 2003.

Nobleman, Marc Tyler. *The Thirteen Colonies.* We the People. Minneapolis: Compass Point Books, 2002.

Whitehurst, Susan. *The Colony of Connecticut.* The Library of the Thirteen Colonies and the Lost Colony. New York: PowerKids Press, 2000.

Index